ITALIAN
EASY
GRAMMAR

LONDON, NEW YORK, MUNICH,
MELBOURNE, AND DELHI

Written by Victoria Duncan

Senior Editor Angela Wilkes
Senior Designer Phil Gamble
Production Editor Tony Phipps, Lucy Sims
Production Controller Mandy Inness
Managing Editor Stephanie Farrow
Managing Art Editor Lee Griffiths
US Editor John Searcy

Language content for DK by G-and-W Publishing.

First American Edition, 2012

Published in the United States by
DK Publishing
375 Hudson Street
New York, New York 10014

12 13 14 15 16 10 9 8 7 6 5 4 3 2 1
001—183055—July/2012

A catalog record for this book is available
from the Library of Congress.

ISBN 978-0-7566-9240-7

Printed and bound in China by
Leo Paper Products LTD

Discover more at
www.dk.com

FOREWORD

Grammar is the basic framework of a language—a set of building blocks that you can assemble in many different ways to make sentences. You can learn how to say things from a phrase book, but if you understand how to put words together yourself, and change them when needed, you can build your own sentences and will soon feel confident speaking Italian.

This book covers all the Italian grammar you need to know in bite-sized learning units. All of the basic parts of speech, such as nouns, pronouns, adjectives, verbs, and adverbs, are clearly defined and there are simple explanations of how to use them. Concise examples of everyday Italian, together with translations in English, show you how each grammar point works in practice. Grammar Guru boxes provide useful tips, and all the key points are summarized in a Recap box at the end of each section. A concise glossary of essential grammar terms at the end of the book provides instant reference whenever you need it.

Whether you are a complete beginner or are hoping to brush up on your rusty language skills, you will find *Italian Easy Grammar* not only a useful teaching aid, but a handy revision guide and an invaluable source of reference.

CONTENTS

NOUNS

GENDER

A noun is a word used to name an object, a person, or an abstract idea, for example *apple*, *John Smith*, or *happiness*. Unlike English, however, all nouns in Italian are either masculine (usually abbreviated to masc.) or feminine (fem.). This is what is known as the gender of a noun.

MASCULINE	FEMININE
libro book	**penna** pen
studente student	**amica** (female) friend
nome name	**tristezza** sadness
uomo man	**donna** woman

IL AND LA (DEFINITE ARTICLE)

The Italian definite article corresponds to the English word *the*. It is different for masculine and feminine nouns. The definite article for a masculine noun is usually **il**, and for a feminine noun it is **la**.

If a masculine noun begins with **z** (e.g. **zero**), or **s** followed by another consonant (e.g. **studente**), then **il** changes to **lo**.

MASCULINE	FEMININE
il libro the book	**la penna** the pen
il nome the name	**la donna** the woman
lo studente the student	**la tristezza** the sadness

Italian nouns have one of three endings: **-o**, **-a**, or **-e**.

❶ If a noun ends in **-o** it is usually masculine, e.g. **il vino** (*wine*), **il biscotto** (*biscuit*).

❷ If a noun ends in **-a** it is usually feminine, e.g. **la birra** (*beer*), **la panna** (*cream*).

❸ If a noun ends in **-e** it can be either masculine, e.g. **il nome** (*name*), or feminine, e.g. **la stazione** (*station*). You will need to learn the gender.

In Italian, the definite article is often used in the same way as in English: to indicate a specific item. So, instead of saying *fish*, you can specify *the fish*. However, Italian also uses the definite article to talk about a noun in a more general sense. This can be confusing to an English speaker, but you will become used to it:

Adoro il vino!	I love wine!
Adriana guarda la televisione	Adriana is watching television
Il gatto attraversa la strada	The cat is crossing the road

UN AND UNA (INDEFINITE ARTICLE)

The indefinite article in Italian is the equivalent of the English *a/an*. The masculine indefinite article is **un**, and the feminine is **una**.

If a masculine noun begins with **z**, or **s** followed by another consonant, **un** changes to **uno**.

MASCULINE	FEMININE
un biscotto a biscuit	**una donna** a woman
un uomo a man	**una penna** a pen
uno studente a student	**una stazione** a station

Cerco un ristorante italiano	I'm looking for an Italian restaurant
È una ragazza intelligente	She's an intelligent girl

GRAMMAR GURU

If a noun begins with a vowel, the definite article is shortened to **l'**, and the feminine indefinite article **una** is shortened to **un'**.

l'uomo (*the man*)

un'amica (*a female friend*)

PLURALS

Nouns can either be singular or plural. If there is only one of the object, or you are talking about the object in a general sense, it is usually singular. If there are multiple objects, the plural is used.

FORMING THE PLURAL

Talking about more than one of an object is often fairly straightforward in English—we usually just add -s or -es to the end of the noun (books, boxes). It is more complicated in Italian, but there are some general rules you can follow:

❶ A singular noun ending in **-o** usually changes to **-i** in the plural: **biscotto/biscotti** (biscuit/biscuits).
❷ A singular noun ending in **-a** usually changes to **-e** in the plural: **penna/penne** (pen/pens).
❸ A singular noun ending in **-e** usually changes to **-i** in the plural: **stazione/stazioni** (station/stations).

DEFINITE ARTICLES IN THE PLURAL

The definite article for masculine plural nouns is usually **i**, and for a feminine nouns it is **le**.

The singular article **lo** (used with words beginning with **z** or **s** + consonant) changes to **gli** in the plural. **Gli** is also used for the plural of masculine nouns starting with a vowel.

SINGULAR	PLURAL
Masculine:	
il libro the book	**i libri** the books
il biscotto the book	**i biscotti** the biscuits
lo studente the student	**gli studenti** the students
l'amico the (male) friend	**gli amici** the friends
Feminine:	
la penna the pen	**le penne** the pens
l'ape the bee	**le api** the bees

I libri sono interessanti	The books are interesting
I biscotti sono buoni	The biscuits are good
Gli studenti hanno fame	The students are hungry ("have hunger")
È sempre bello vedere gli amici	It's always nice to see friends
Gli zaini dei bambini sono troppo pesanti	The children's backpacks are too heavy
Le penne qui non funzionano	The pens here don't work
Le spremute sono eccellenti lì	The fresh juices are excellent there
Ho pulito tutte le tavole	I have cleaned all the tables

There are some plural nouns that do not follow regular patterns. A good dictionary will tell you how to form the plural of each, so check if you are unsure.

TO RECAP

- Italian nouns are either masculine or feminine.
- Nouns ending in -o are usually masculine, -a are usually feminine, and -e can be either.
- The definite article (*the*) is usually **il** for masculine singular nouns, **la** for feminine singular nouns, **i** for masculine plural, and **le** for feminine plural.
- The indefinite article (*a/an*) is usually **un** for masculine nouns and **una** for feminine nouns.
- Plurals in Italian are made by changing the ending of a noun: -o or -e usually change to -i; -a usually changes to -e.

PRONOUNS

A pronoun tells you who did something (the subject of a sentence), for example *I threw the ball* or <u>he</u> *rang yesterday*. Grammatically this is important to know, as verbs in Italian change depending on the subject of the sentence.

io	I
tu	you (informal)
Lei	you (formal)
lui	he
lei	she
noi	we
voi	you (plural)
loro	they

Pronouns are often not used in Italian, as the verb ending will usually tell you who or what is the subject of the sentence. Pronouns are, however, often used to clarify or emphasize a point, as in the examples below.

Io parlo italiano ma lui non parla italiano	I speak Italian but <u>he</u> doesn't speak Italian
Noi volevamo venire ma lui non ha tempo	We wanted to come but he doesn't have time
Io non sono stanca, e tu?	I'm not tired, are you?
Lui mangia la pizza; lei mangia un panino	He's having pizza; she's having a roll

DIFFERENT WAYS OF SAYING YOU

Tu is an informal way of saying *you* in Italian. It is always singular. If you're addressing someone more formally, you should use **Lei** and the same form of a verb that you use for *he* or *she*. Although **lei** also means *she*, it can be used for men or women when it means *you*.

Voi is generally used to address a group of people as *you*. As explained on page 10, using a pronoun is not usually necessary, so they are shown in brackets in the examples below:

(Tu) parli inglese?	Do you speak English? (*informal*)
(Lei) parla inglese?	Do you speak English? (*formal*)
(Voi) parlate inglese?	Do you speak English? (*plural*)

Although **voi** is generally used to address a group of people as *you*, employees in restaurants or hotels sometimes use **Loro**, the plural of the formal **Lei**, when they are being deferential.

(Loro) prendono un aperitivo?	Are you having an aperitif?
(Loro) hanno prenotato?	Have you booked?

GRAMMAR GURU

Italians sometimes use **si** (literally meaning *one*) to generalize about something, for example **si mangia** (*one eats*), or **si dorme** (*one sleeps*), or occasionally where in English *we* would be used:

Che si fa stasera?	What shall we do tonight?

POSSESSIVES

Possessives and demonstratives are really adjectives (see pp.14-19), but it is useful to look at them together with nouns and pronouns.

Possessives tell you who owns something and are the equivalent of the English *my, your,* etc. In Italian, they change depending on the item(s) owned.

Each Italian possessive has four alternatives depending on whether the noun following it is masculine, feminine, or plural, for example: **il mio libro** (*my book*), **la mia penna** (*my pen*), **i miei libri** (*my books*), **le mie penne** (*my pens*).

MASC.	FEM.	M. PL.	F. PL.	TRANSLATION
il mio	la mia	i miei	le mie	my
il tuo	la tua	i tuoi	le tue	your (informal)
il suo	la sua	i suoi	le sue	his/her/your (for.)
il nostro	la nostra	i nostri	le nostre	our
il vostro	la vostra	i vostri	le vostre	your (pl.)
il loro	la loro	i loro	le loro	their

La mia amica abita a Roma	My (female) friend lives in Rome
I nostri genitori sono in vacanza	Our parents are on vacation
Aldo ha perso il suo cellulare	Aldo has lost his cell phone

GRAMMAR GURU

Generally the possessives in Italian consist of two words, e.g. **il mio** (literally meaning "*the my*"). But when you talk about individual members of the family, you don't need to include *the*:

mio fratello/mia sorella   my brother/my sister

DEMONSTRATIVES

Demonstratives (*this*, *these*, *that*, and *those*) specify which noun you are talking about. The words for them change in Italian, depending on the gender and the number of the noun referred to.

THIS AND THESE

	MASC.	FEM.	TRANSLATION
SING.	questo	questa	this
PLURAL	questi	queste	these

THAT AND THOSE

	MASC.	FEM.	TRANSLATION
SING.	quel	quella	this
	quello	quell'	
	quell'		
PLURAL	quei	quelle	those
	quegli		

Quel and **quei** are used before most masculine nouns starting with a consonant, apart from **z**, **gn**, **pn**, **ps**, **x**, and **s** + another consonant. **Quello** and **quegli** are used before these. **Quell'** is used before all nouns that begin with a vowel.

questo libro	this book
questa casa	this house
questi studenti	these students
queste patate	these potatoes
quel gatto	that cat
quella casa	that house
quegli studenti	those students

ADJECTIVES

Adjectives are words used to describe something, for example *green* or *beautiful*. In Italian, an adjective changes according to the number and gender of what it describes (generally referred to as agreement).

ADJECTIVES ENDING IN -O

Most adjectives in Italian end in **-o** when referring to a masculine singular noun. They change as follows:

GENDER	NUMBER	AGREEMENT
masculine	singular	-o
feminine	singular	-a
masculine	plural	-i
feminine	plural	-e

Adjectives that follow this pattern are very common. **Nero** (*black*) is one such adjective:

Il gatto è nero	The cat is black
La penna è nera	The pen is black
I gatti sono neri	The cats are black
Le penne sono nere	The pens are black

It is important to note that an **-e** on the end of an Italian word should be pronounced separately, so **nere** is pronounced "*neray*."

In a dictionary, most Italian adjectives are shown in the masculine singular form. You will need to add the correct ending for feminine and plural adjectives.

Here are some common adjectives that end in -**o**:

bello	beautiful
caro	expensive
piccolo	small
buono	good, tasty
freddo	cold
caldo	hot
rumoroso	noisy
Questi biscotti sono buoni	These biscuits are good
La mia minestra è fredda	My soup is cold
La camera è bella	The room is beautiful
Quegli studenti sono rumorosi	Those students are noisy
Questa casa è piccola	This house is small
Il ristorante è caro	The restaurant is expensive
Le ragazze sono pigre	The girls are lazy

GRAMMAR GURU

The endings of Italian nouns and adjectives vary according to gender. They often match, e.g. **il gatto è nero**, but the endings can also differ:

Il violinista è bravo	The violinist is great
La stazione è rumorosa	The station is noisy
La mano è piccola	The hand is small

ADJECTIVES ENDING IN -E

Some Italian adjectives end in **-e**. They don't change for the feminine, only for the plural:

GENDER	NUMBER	AGREEMENT
masculine	singular	-e
feminine	singular	-e
masculine	plural	-i
feminine	plural	-i

Questo libro è divertente	This book is funny
Il treno è veloce	The train is fast
Gli alberghi sono inglesi	The hotels are English
Anna è molto intelligente	Anna is very intelligent
Vorrei due camere grandi	I would like two large rooms

WORD ORDER WITH ADJECTIVES

In Italian, adjectives are usually placed after the thing they describe:

un libro divertente	an amusing book
una camera piccola	a small room
Dove sono le mie scarpe nere?	Where are my black shoes?

However, sometimes you may see an adjective before the noun. This might subtly change the meaning. Examples of adjectives used in this way are:

buono	good, tasty
grande	big, large
vecchio	old
bello	beautiful
un amico vecchio	an old (elderly) friend
un vecchio amico	an old friend (I've known for a long time)
un uomo grande	a large man
un grande uomo	an important man

COLORS

Although most color adjectives follow the regular patterns, a few don't change at all:

COLOR	SINGULAR	PLURAL
blue	**blu**	**blu**
purple	**viola**	**viola**
pink	**rosa**	**rosa**
brown	**marrone**	**marrone**
lilac	**lilla**	**lilla**

una borsa marrone	a brown bag
delle scarpe marrone	some brown shoes
un vestito blu	a blue dress
una camicia rosa	a pink shirt
degli stivali viola	some purple boots

TO RECAP

- Italian adjectives usually change according to gender (masc./fem.) and number (sing./pl.).
- Most adjectives are put after the noun but some are placed before it.

COMPARATIVES

Adjectives can be used in a comparative structure
to differentiate between two or more things.
To say *more than*, use the construction **più...di...**:

Questo vestito è più bello di quello	This dress is nicer than that one
Giovanni è più sportivo di Daniele	Giovanni is sportier than Daniele

To say *less than*, use the construction **meno...di...**:

La politica è meno interessante dell'arte	Politics is less interesting than art
Il pecorino fresco è meno piccante del pecorino maturo	Fresh pecorino is less strong (tasting) than mature pecorino

To describe two things as equal, use **come**:

Ugo è intelligente come Elisa	Ugo is as intelligent as Elisa
Cristiana è gentile come Franca	Cristiana is as kind as Franca

GRAMMAR GURU

You can also compare two qualities or characteristics
by changing **di** to **che** in the comparative structure
più...che.../meno...che...:

Mio figlio è più intelligente che studioso	My son is more intelligent than studious
È meno difficile dire che fare	It's less difficult to say than to do

SUPERLATIVES

The comparative construction can also be used to talk about superiority (the most) or inferiority (the least). This is known as the superlative.

The Italian definite article (the) and the adjective both change according to the gender and number of the thing described:

il/la/i/le + più + adjective = the most

il/la/i/le + meno + adjective = the least

il libro meno interessante	the least interesting book
la pizza più deliziosa	the most delicious pizza
le camere più piccole	the smallest rooms
gli alberghi più grandi	the biggest hotels

BETTER/BEST; WORSE/WORST

The Italian for better/the best and worse/the worst are irregular, as they are in English.

	COMPARATIVE	SUPERLATIVE
buono good	migliore/migliori better (sing./pl.)	il/la/i/le migliore/-i the best
cattivo bad	peggiore/peggiori worse	il/la/i/le peggiore/-i the worst

Vuole la camera migliore	He wants the best room
Il mio cellulare è peggiore del tuo	My cell phone is worse than yours

THE INFINITIVE

Verbs are often called action words or doing words. They describe what someone or something is doing, for example *run, jump,* or *study.* They can also describe a state rather than a particular action, for example *have* or *be.*

The infinitive is the basic form of a verb and the one you will find in a dictionary. In English it usually has *to* in front of it, for example *to speak.*

DIFFERENT TYPES OF INFINITIVE

Infinitives in Italian usually have one of three endings: **-are, -ere,** or **-ire.** These endings determine how you use (conjugate) the verb.

❶ **-are** ending:

mangiare	to eat
parlare	to talk
imparare	to learn

❷ **-ere** ending:

prendere	to take
vendere	to sell
correre	to run

❸ **-ire** ending:

dormire	to sleep
finire	to finish
preferire	to prefer

WHEN TO USE THE INFINITIVE

There are several ways the infinitive can be used.
One of the most common is as a second verb
following expressions such as **vorrei** (*I would like*)
or **bisogna** (*it is necessary*):

Vorrei parlare con il gestore	I would like to talk to the manager
Bisogna pagare per entrare	It is necessary to pay to enter
Lisa vuole ballare	Lisa wants to dance

The infinitive is also used in Italian after a
preposition such as **a** or **per** (see pp. 48–49
to find out more about prepositions).

Angelo è andato a fare una passeggiata	Angelo has gone for a walk
Sono qui per pranzare	I am here to eat lunch

In Italian, the infinitive can also be used as a noun
to describe an action in general:

Mi piace ballare	I like dancing
Imparare l'italiano non è difficile	Learning Italian isn't difficult

TO RECAP

- The infinitive is the basic form of a verb.
- It can be used as a second verb or after a preposition.
- The infinitive is also used as a noun to describe an action in general terms.

THE PRESENT TENSE

The present tense is used in Italian to talk about what is happening now, and also to describe what happens regularly:

Cristiana va a scuola ora	Cristiana is going to school now
Cristiana va a scuola ogni giorno	Cristiana goes to school every day

Most verbs change according to who or what is carrying out the action (the subject). These changes are known as conjugation. Regular verbs change according to whether the infinitive ends in **-are**, **-ere**, or **-ire** (see pp.20–21).

To conjugate a regular verb, you need to remove the last three letters of the infinitive and add the endings shown in the following lists.

REGULAR -ARE VERBS

The endings for regular **-are** verbs (e.g. **parlare**) are shown underlined in the list below:

(io) parlo	I talk
(tu) parli	you (sing. informal) talk
(Lei) parla	you (sing. formal) talk
(lui) parla	he talks
(lei) parla	she talks
(noi) parliamo	we talk
(voi) parlate	you (plural) talk
(loro) parlano	they talk

Parlo con mia madre ogni giorno	I speak to my mother every day
Luigi impara l'inglese	Luigi is learning English
I miei figli abitano a Londra	My children live in London

REGULAR -ERE VERBS

To conjugate a regular verb ending in **-ere** (e.g. **prendere**), remove the last three letters of the infinitive and add the endings underlined below:

(io) prend**o**	I take
(tu) prend**i**	you (sing. informal) take
(Lei) prend**e**	you (sing. formal) take
(lui) prend**e**	he takes
(lei) prend**e**	she takes
(noi) prend**iamo**	we take
(voi) prend**ete**	you (plural) take
(loro) prend**ono**	they take
Prendiamo un caffè nel giardino	We're having a coffee in the garden
Vedo la mia insegnante ogni giorno	I see my teacher every day
Vendono la loro casa	They're selling their house

GRAMMAR GURU

Traditionally the formal word for *you*, **Lei**, is written with a capital letter to distinguish it from **lei** meaning *she*. These days, however, you will often see both of them written without a capital.

REGULAR -IRE VERBS

Verbs ending in -ire divide into two groups.

❶ -ire group 1 (e.g. dormire):

(io) dorm<u>o</u>	I sleep
(tu) dorm<u>i</u>	you (sing. informal) sleep
(Lei) dorm<u>e</u>	you (sing. formal) sleep
(lui) dorm<u>e</u>	he sleeps
(lei) dorm<u>e</u>	she sleeps
(noi) dorm<u>iamo</u>	we sleep
(voi) dorm<u>ite</u>	you (plural) sleep
(loro) dorm<u>ono</u>	they sleep
Dormiamo sempre fino a tardi	We always sleep late
Parto alle otto	I'm leaving at eight

❷ -ire group 2 (e.g. finire):

(io) fin<u>isco</u>	I finish
(tu) fin<u>isci</u>	you (sing. informal) finish
(Lei) fin<u>isce</u>	you (sing. formal) finish
(lui) fin<u>isce</u>	he finishes
(lei) fin<u>isce</u>	she finishes
(noi) fin<u>iamo</u>	we finish
(voi) fin<u>ite</u>	you (plural) finish
(loro) fin<u>iscono</u>	they finish
Preferisce la carne o il pesce?	Do you prefer fish or meat?
Di solito finisco presto	I usually finish quickly

FORMING THE NEGATIVE

To make a verb negative in Italian (to say that something is <u>not</u> happening), you put **non** directly in front of the verb:

Non vendiamo la nostra casa	We're not selling our house
Non fumo	I don't smoke

Other negative meanings can be produced by using **non**, then adding a more specific word directly after the verb:

non...mai	never/not ever
non...nessuno	no one/not anyone
non...niente	nothing/not anything
non...più	no longer/not anymore

Giorgio non finisce mai i suoi compiti	Giorgio never finishes his homework
Non aspettiamo nessuno	We're not waiting for anyone
Non c'è niente da fare	There's nothing to do
Non lavoro più	I don't work anymore

TO RECAP

- The present tense is used to describe current or habitual actions.
- Verbs are divided into four categories according to infinitive: **-are**; **-ere**; **-ire** group 1; **-ire** group 2.
- Regular verbs are conjugated by adding different endings to the infinitive minus the final three letters.
- The negative is formed by putting **non** directly before the verb.

IRREGULAR VERBS

Not all verbs are regular in the present tense.
Some are irregular in a reasonably predictable way,
but others don't appear to follow any recognizable
pattern at all and must simply he learned.

Some of the most common Italian verbs are
irregular. Probably the three most important are
essere (*to be*), **avere** (*to have*), and **andare** (*to go*).
The present tenses of **essere** and **avere** are also
used to form one of the past tenses in Italian.

ESSERE (TO BE)

The verb **essere** (*to be*) in the present tense is
essential and needs to be learned by heart.

(io) sono	I am
(tu) sei	you (sing. informal) are
(Lei) è	you (sing. formal) are
(lui) è	he is
(lei) è	she is
(noi) siamo	we are
(voi) siete	you (plural) are
(loro) sono	they are
Sono francese	I'm French
È mio fratello	He's my brother
Sono gentili	They're kind
Non siamo stanchi	We're not tired
Lei è Franca Barnato?	Are you Franca Barnato?

AVERE (TO HAVE)

(io) ho	I have
(tu) hai	you (sing. informal) have
(Lei) ha	you (sing. formal) have
(lui) ha	he has
(lei) ha	she has
(noi) abbiamo	we have
(voi) avete	you (plural) have
(loro) hanno	they have
Ho una macchina verde	I have a green car
Hai fame?	Are you hungry? (Do you have hunger?)
Non hanno un cane	They don't have a dog
Maria ha un vestito carino	Maria has a pretty dress

GRAMMAR GURU

To say *there is* in Italian you use the phrase **c'è**. In the plural this changes to **ci sono** (*there are*). The negative is **non c'è/non ci sono** (*there isn't/there aren't*).

C'è un mercato qui il giovedì	There's a market here on Thursdays
Ci sono due tavole prenotate per noi	There are two tables booked for us
Non c'è latte	There isn't any milk
Non ci sono abbastanza sedie	There aren't enough chairs

ANDARE (TO GO)

Only the forms of the verb **andare** for **noi** and **voi** follow a regular pattern; the rest of the present tense is irregular:

(io) vado	I go
(tu) vai	you (sing. informal) go
(Lei) va	you (sing. formal) go
(lui) va	he goes
(lei) va	she goes
(noi) andiamo	we go
(voi) andate	you (plural) go
(loro) vanno	they go
Vado a Roma	I'm going to Rome
Vanno insieme in piscina	They are going together to the swimming pool
Andate alla festa di Giacomo?	Are you going to Giacomo's party?
Carlo va alla stessa scuola del mio amico	Carlo goes to the same school as my friend
Non andiamo a Siena questo fine settimana	We're not going to Siena this weekend

GRAMMAR GURU

The infinitive **andare** (*to go*), and the parts of the verb used for **noi** and **voi**, don't seem to bear any resemblance at all to the other parts of the conjugation (**vado, vai, va, vanno**). The theory is that the present tense of the Italian verb **andare** is derived from two entirely different Latin verbs: **ambulare** (*to walk*) and **vadere** (*to go*).

OTHER IRREGULAR VERBS

Here are a few of the more common irregular Italian verbs:

FARE (TO MAKE/TO DO)

The Italian verb **fare** is used in many different ways.

(io) faccio	I make/do
(tu) fai	you (sing. inf.) make/do
(Lei) fa	you (sing. for.) make/do
(lui/lei) fa	he/she makes/does
(noi) facciamo	we make/do
(voi) fate	you (plural) make/do
(loro) fanno	they make/do
Che lavoro fa?	What (job) do you do?
Cosa fanno?	What are they doing?
Facciamo tutto noi stessi	We make everything ourselves

DARE (TO GIVE)

(io) do	I give
(tu) dai	you (sing. informal) give
(Lei) da	you (sing. formal) give
(lui/lei) da	he/she gives
(noi) diamo	we give
(voi) date	you (plural) give
(loro) danno	they give
Laura da il libro a Ugo	Laura's giving the book to Ugo

POTERE (TO BE ABLE TO/CAN)

(io) posso	I am able to/can
(tu) puoi	you (sing. informal) can
(Lei) può	you (sing. formal) can
(lui/lei) può	he/she can
(noi) possiamo	we can
(voi) potete	you (plural) can
(loro) possono	they can
Può aprire la porta?	Can you open the door?
Non posso uscire	I can't go out

VOLERE (TO WANT)

(io) voglio	I want
(tu) vuoi	you (sing. informal) want
(Lei) vuole	you (sing. formal) want
(lui/lei) vuole	he/she wants
(noi) vogliamo	we want
(voi) volete	you (plural) want
(loro) vogliono	they want
Paolo vuole partire	Paolo wants to leave
Non volete mangiare?	Don't you want to eat?

GRAMMAR GURU

It can seem rude to request something using **voglio** (*I want*). In general, it is more polite to use **vorrei** (*I would like*):

Vorrei un cappuccino per favore	I would like a cappuccino, please

BERE (TO DRINK)

(io) bevo	I drink
(tu) bevi	you (sing. informal) drink
(Lei) beve	you (sing. formal) drink
(lui/lei) beve	he/she drinks
(noi) beviamo	we drink
(voi) bevete	you (plural) drink
(loro) bevono	they drink
Bevete qualcosa?	Would you like something to drink?
Non bevo alcool	I don't drink alcohol
Le ragazze bevono troppa cola	The girls drink too much cola
Lui beve il caffè ma noi beviamo il tè	He drinks coffee but we drink tea

TO RECAP

- Many verbs in Italian do not follow a regular pattern in the present tense, so it is best to learn them individually.
- The verbs **essere** (to be), **avere** (to have), and **andare** (to go) are important irregular verbs to learn.
- Some irregular verbs are are conjugated in a similar way.
- Other irregular verbs are more individual and need to be learned by heart.
- To like is expressed in Italian by using the phrase **mi piace** "it pleases me," **ti piace** "it pleases you," **le piace** "it pleases her" etc.

THE PERFECT TENSE

The perfect tense is used to describe events in the past that have been completed. It is made up of two parts:

❶ The present tense of **avere** (or sometimes **essere**).

❷ The past participle of the verb you are using, e.g. **mangiare** (*to eat*).

Aldo ha mangiato un panino	Aldo ate/has eaten a sandwich
Abbiamo mangiato della pizza	We ate/have eaten pizza

THE PAST PARTICIPLE

Past participles are the equivalent of the English words *eaten*, *bought*, etc. To form the past participle of a verb, take the infinitive and remove the last three letters. You then add **-ato** for a verb ending in **-are**, so that **mangiare** (*to eat*) becomes **mangiato** (*eaten*).

(io) ho mangiato	I ate/have eaten
(tu) hai mangiato	you (inf.) ate/have eaten
(Lei) ha mangiato	you (for.) ate/have eaten
(lui) ha mangiato	he ate/has eaten
(lei) ha mangiato	she ate/has eaten
(noi) abbiamo mangiato	we ate/have eaten
(voi) avete mangiato	you (pl.) ate/have eaten
(loro) hanno mangiato	they ate/have eaten

The past participles of verbs ending in **-ere**, such as **vendere**, are formed in the same way, but you replace the last three letters of the infinitive with

-uto, so **vendere** (*to sell*) becomes **venduto** (*sold*):
ho venduto (*I sold/have sold*), etc.

The past participles of verbs ending in -**ire** ,
such as **finire**, are formed in the same way but
you replace the last three letters of the infinitive
with -**ito**, so **finire** (*to finish*) becomes **finito**
(*finished*): **ho finito** (*I finished/have finished*), etc.

Hai mangiato da Piero?	Did you eat at Piero's?
Maria ha finito i suoi compiti	Maria has finished her homework
Hanno venduto la loro casa	They sold their house

IRREGULAR VERBS

Some past participles in Italian do not follow
these rules, so it is best to learn them by heart.
Below are some common examples:

INFINITIVE	TRANSLATION	PAST PARTICIPLE
aprire	to open	**aperto**
bere	to drink	**bevuto**
chiedere	to ask	**chiesto**
dire	to say	**detto**
fare	to make/to do	**fatto**
perdere	to lose	**perso**
prendere	to take	**preso**
rompere	to break	**rotto**
vedere	to see	**visto**

Avete perso la chiave?	Have you lost the key?
Abbiamo bevuto il vino	We drank the wine

THE PERFECT TENSE USING ESSERE

Some verbs are formed in the perfect tense by using **essere** (*to be*, see p. 26) instead of **avere**. One of the most important of these is **andare** (*to go*):

(io) sono andato	I went/have gone
(tu) sei andato	you (inf.) went/have gone
(Lei) è andato	you (for.) went/have gone
(lui) è andato	he went/has gone
(lei) è andata	she went/has gone
(noi) siamo andati	we went/have gone
(voi) siete andati	you (pl.) went/have gone
(loro) sono andati	they went/have gone

Other common verbs that also use **essere** are:

INFINITIVE	TRANSLATION	PAST PARTICIPLE
venire	to come	venuto
uscire	to go out	uscito
stare	to stay	stato
entrare	to enter	entrato
partire	to leave	partito
diventare	to become	diventato

GRAMMAR GURU

If the subject is female and the verb uses **essere** in the past tense, the final -**o** on the end of the past participle changes to -**a**. In a similar way, the final -**o** changes to -**i** if the subject is masculine plural, or -**e** if it is feminine plural:

Caterina è andata a Londra	Caterina went to London
Sono venuti ieri sera	They came yesterday evening

Siamo andati a Venezia insieme	We went to Venice together
Lisa è venuta dopo un viaggio di due ore	She came after a two hour journey
Mio fratello è partito dieci minuti fa	My brother left ten minutes ago
La benzina è diventata molto più cara	Gasoline has become much more expensive

THE PERFECT TENSE NEGATIVE

The negative of the perfect tense is formed by putting **non** in front of **avere** (or **essere**), rather than in front of the past participle:

non + **avere/essere** + past participle

Non ho visto il mare	I didn't see the sea
Non sono venuti da noi questa settimana	They didn't come to us this week
Non siete usciti ieri sera?	Didn't you go out yesterday evening?
Non hai detto niente a nessuno, vero?	You didn't tell anyone, did you?

TO RECAP

- The perfect tense is used to describe completed events.
- The tense is formed with the present tense of **avere** (or **essere**) + a past participle.
- The past participle of regular verbs is made by replacing -**are** with -**ato**, -**ere** with -**uto**, and -**ire** with -**ito**. Some past participles are irregular.
- The negative is formed by making **avere** (or **essere**) negative and then adding the participle.

THE IMPERFECT TENSE

The perfect tense (see pp.34–37) is used to talk about events in the past that have been completed. However, if you want to describe what things were like in the past you need to use the imperfect tense, for example, I was unhappy; we were living in Italy; you were waiting at the bus stop.

FORMING THE IMPERFECT

In general, you remove the last two letters of the infinitive and add the endings underlined below:

(io) abita<u>vo</u>	I was living
(tu) abita<u>vi</u>	you (inf.) were living
(Lei) abita<u>va</u>	you (for.) were living
(lui) abita<u>va</u>	he was living
(lei) abita<u>va</u>	she was living
(noi) abita<u>vamo</u>	we were living
(voi) abita<u>vate</u>	you (plural) were living
(loro) abita<u>vano</u>	they were living

Abitavate a Roma lo scorso anno?	Were you living in Rome last year?
Non mi sentivo bene ieri	I wasn't feeling well yesterday
La famiglia Medici veniva da Firenze	The Medici family came (was coming) from Venice
Aspettavamo l'autobus quando è passato il mio amico	We were waiting for the bus when my friend passed by

WAS/WERE

Essere (*to be*, see p.26) is irregular but is a very useful verb to learn for describing things in the past:

(io) ero	I was
(tu) eri	you (sing. informal) were
(Lei) era	you (sing. formal) were
(lui) era	he was
(lei) era	she was
(noi) eravamo	we were
(voi) eravate	you (plural) were
(loro) erano	they were
La macchina era bella ma troppo cara	The car was beautiful, but too expensive
Eravate molto contenti qui?	Were you very happy here?
La mostra era favolosa	The exhibition was superb
Erano troppo giovani per questo film	They were too young for this movie

GRAMMAR GURU

If you want to talk about the weather in the past, Italian uses **faceva** (*it was doing*) rather than **era** (*it was*):

Faceva bel tempo a Sestri Levante	The weather was lovely in Sestri Levante
Ieri faceva freddo a Genova	Yesterday it was cold in Genoa
Faceva brutto tempo il fine settimana	The weather was bad last weekend

THE FUTURE TENSE

FORMING THE FUTURE TENSE

The future tense is generally formed by removing
the final -e of the infinitive and adding the endings
underlined below. Be careful to emphasize the
future endings when you pronounce the verb.

(io) partirò	I'll leave
(tu) partirai	you'll (informal) leave
(Lei) partirà	you'll (formal) leave
(lui) partirà	he'll leave
(lei) partirà	she'll leave
(noi) partiremo	we'll leave
(voi) partirete	you'll (plural) leave
(loro) partiranno	they'll leave

There is a small spelling change in future verbs
formed from -**are** infinitives, with the **a** changing
to an e: for example **comprare** (*to buy*) becomes
comprerò (*I'll buy*).

Aspetteranno una mezz'ora	They'll wait for half an hour
Vittoria partirà dopo colazione	Vittoria will leave after breakfast
La settimana prossima comprerò una nuova bicicletta	Next week I'll buy a new bicycle
Compreremo un giornale in città	We'll buy a newspaper in town
Finirò di fare i compiti fra dieci minuti	I will finish my homework in ten minutes

GRAMMAR GURU

A few commonly used verbs drop one or two letters from the infinitive when the future endings are added. For example, **andare** (*to go*) becomes **andrò** (*I'll go*) and **vedere** (*to see*) becomes **vedremo** (*we'll see*).

WILL BE

The future tense of the verb **essere** follows a different pattern:

(io) sarò	I'll be
(tu) sarai	you'll (informal) be
(Lei) sarà	you'll (formal) be
(lui) sarà	he'll be
(lei) sarà	she'll be
(noi) saremo	we'll be
(voi) sarete	you'll (plural) be
(loro) saranno	they'll be
Come sarai stanca domani mattina!	You'll be so tired tomorrow morning!
Sarà bello vedervi	It willl be nice to see you
I biscotti saranno pronti fra poco	The biscuits will be ready soon

TO RECAP

- The future tense is made by adding specific endings to a shortened infinitive.
- There are some minor spelling changes to certain verbs when the future endings are added.
- The future of **essere** is irregular and needs to be learned.

REFLEXIVE VERBS

Reflexive verbs are often used to talk about an action that you do to yourself, for example **(io) mi lavo** (*I wash myself*). There are some reflexive verbs in Italian that are not obviously about an action to yourself, for example **(io) mi chiamo** (*my name is*).

USING REFLEXIVE VERBS

Reflexive verbs follow the normal verb patterns, but include a reflexive pronoun before the verb:

SUBJECT	REFLEXIVE PRON.	EXAMPLE
io (*I*)	mi	mi lavo
tu (*you, inf.*)	ti	ti lavi
Lei (*you, for.*)	si	si lava
lui (*he*)	si	si lava
lei (*she*)	si	si lava
noi (*we*)	ci	ci laviamo
voi (*you, pl.*)	vi	vi lavate
loro (*they*)	si	si lavano

Si chiamano Silvia e Alessia	Their names are Silvia and Alessia
Mi lavo prima di andare a letto	I wash before going to bed
A che ora ti svegli?	What time do you wake up?
Elisabetta si trucca prima di uscire	Elisabetta puts on makeup before going out
Non si sente bene oggi	He doesn't feel well today
Ci divertiamo sempre a Capodanno	We always enjoy ourselves at New Year's

REFLEXIVE VERBS IN THE PERFECT TENSE

Reflexive verbs all use **essere** in the perfect tense (see pp.36-37). To form the perfect tense of a reflexive verb, put the appropriate form of **essere** between the reflexive pronoun and the past participle, for example **mi sono lavato** (*I washed myself*):

perfect tense reflexive =
reflexive pronoun + **essere** + past participle

Si è svegliato alle cinque questa mattina	He woke up at five o'clock this morning
Mi sono divertita molto ieri sera	I really enjoyed myself yesterday evening
Si sono lavati prima di mangiare	They washed before eating

REFLEXIVES IN THE NEGATIVE

In the negative form, **non** comes before the reflexive pronoun but after the subject:

Non mi alzo tardi	I don't get up late
Mio fratello non si rade mai	My brother never shaves
Non ci siamo divertiti alla festa	We didn't enjoy the party

GRAMMAR GURU

Don't forget, the past participles of verbs using **essere** in the perfect tense change according to gender and number (see Grammar Guru, p.36). Since reflexive verbs use **essere** in the perfect, the ending of the participle changes for feminine and plural subjects:

Emilia si è alzata alle dieci, ma noi ci siamo alzati più presto	Emilia got up at ten o'clock, but we got up earlier

ADVERBS

Adverbs are used to describe a verb. In the sentence *Paul runs quickly*, for example, *quickly* is an adverb and describes how Paul runs. Adverbs can be used to talk about the time and place of the action, and can also describe adjectives or other adverbs, as in the case of *very* in the sentence *Paul runs very quickly*. Unlike adjectives, Italian adverbs do not change their form according to gender or number.

ADVERBS OF MANNER

These are used to describe an action. Most Italian adverbs like this are formed by removing the final letter of the adjective and adding **-amente: lento/lentamente** (*slow/slowly*), or **-emente: triste/tristemente** (*sad/sadly*). For adjectives ending in **-le** or **-re** you still remove the final letter but replace it with only **-mente: facile/facilmente** (*easy/easily*); **particolare/particolarmente** (*particular/particularly*).

Sono completamente esaurita	I'm completely exhausted
Il castello non è particolarmente grande	The castle isn't particularly big

IRREGULAR ADVERBS

Some common adverbs are irregular, or are not formed from an adjective, so it is best to learn them by heart. The most useful ones are:

troppo	too much
molto	a lot/very
poco	a little
bene	well

male	badly
meglio	better
peggio	worse

ADVERBS OF TIME

These adverbs tell you when something happened and usually go directly after a verb, e.g.:

dopo	after
ieri	yesterday
fra poco	soon
già	already
ora	now
spesso	often
sempre	always, still
Claudio va spesso alla piscina	Claudio often goes to the swimming pool
Andiamo fra poco	We're going soon

ADVERBS OF PLACE

These adverbs tell you where something is happening, e.g.:

vicino	nearby
lontano	far away
fuori	outside
qui	here
là	there
dovunque	everywhere
Non abito qui; abito qui vicino	I don't live here; I live nearby

CONJUNCTIONS

A conjunction is a word that joins together parts of a sentence, for example *and*, *but*, *so*, or *because*.

BASIC CONJUNCTIONS

Below is a list of the most basic conjunctions for linking elements in a sentence.

e	and
o	or
ma	but
così	so
poi	then/later
perché	because
comunque	however
Mi piacciono il pecorino e il parmigiano	I like pecorino and parmesan
Vuoi andare alla piscina o al cinema?	Do you want to go to the pool or the movies?
Siamo in vacanza ma dobbiamo lavorare	We are on vacation but we have to work
Non vengo perché sto male	I'm not coming because I don't feel well
Non ne ha voglia, comunque verrà	He doesn't feel like it; however he will come
Non c'era più aranciata così abbiamo comprato della limonata	There wasn't any more orangeade so we bought lemonade

VERBS FOLLOWED BY DI

VERB WITH DI	TRANSLATION
avere bisogno di	to need ("have need of")
smettere di	to stop
essere contento di	to be happy with/to
ridere di	to laugh at
ricordarsi di	to remember
sapere di	to taste of

Ha bisogno d'un consiglio	She needs advice
Ti ricordi di me?	Do you remember me?
Saremo contenti di incontrarvi	We will be happy to meet you
Ho smesso di fumare	I've stopped smoking
Non ridere di me!	Don't laugh at me!
Questo vino sa di fragole	This wine tastes of strawberries
Abbiamo bisogno d'un sacchetto	We need a small bag

TO RECAP

- Prepositions are words describing position or the relationship of different words to each other.
- Some prepositions merge with the definite article in particular instances.
- Prepositions are commonly associated with verbs in Italian. The preposition used may be the same as the one that is used in English, or different from it.

FORMING QUESTIONS

Turning a statement into a question is straightforward in Italian.

QUESTIONING TONE

To form a question, simply say the statement with a questioning tone:

Abramo ha una sorella	Abramo has a sister
Abramo ha una sorella?	Does Abramo have a sister?
Non abitate a Roma	You don't live in Rome
Non abitate a Roma?	Don't you live in Rome?

SHORT ANSWERS

Italian uses a variety of short answers that are the equivalent of the English *Yes, I do* or *No, I don't*.

The question **hai/ha…?** (*do you have…?*), can be answered with **sì, ce l'ho** or **no, non ce l'ho**.

Hai la tua borsa?	Do you have your bag?
Sì, ce l'ho	Yes, I do
Ha il modulo con Lei?	Do you have the form with you?
Mi dispiace, non ce l'ho	Sorry, no I don't

To say that you know or don't know something, Italian uses **lo so** or **non lo so**.

Quando partiremo?	When do we leave?
Mi dispiace, non lo so	Sorry, I don't know
Papà viene tra poco	Dad's coming soon
Lo so	I know

QUESTION WORDS

Below is a list of common words used to ask more specific questions:

Dove?	Where?
Quando?	When?
Che cosa?	What?
Chi?	Who?
Come?	How?
Perché?	Why?
Quanto?	How much?
Quanti?	How many?
Quale?	Which?, What?
Dove va?	Where are you going?
Come va?	How's it going?
Che cosa hanno visto ieri?	What did they see yesterday?
Quanti anni hai?	How old are you?
Chi viene a pranzare?	Who's coming to lunch?
Quanto vino dobbiamo comprare?	How much wine do we have to buy?

GRAMMAR GURU

The last three words in the list above change depending on the gender and/or number of the noun that follows, for example **Quanto pane?** (*How much bread?*) but **Quanta frutta?** (*How much fruit?*); **Quanti panini?** (*How many sandwiches?*) but **Quante mele?** (*How many apples?*); **Quale casa?** (*which house?*) but **Quali case?** (*which houses?*).

DOV'È?

When the question word **dove** (*where*) is written in front of **è** (*is*) the combination becomes **dov'è**. When speaking, you won't hear any difference in the pronunciation of **dove** and **dov'è**:

Dove abita?	Where do you live?
Dov'è il bagno?	Where is the bathroom?
Dove sono le mie valige?	Where are my suitcases?

PERCHÉ?

The word **perché** means both *why* and *because* in Italian:

Perché impara l'italiano	Why are you learning Italian?
Perché mia madre è italiana	Because my mother is Italian

CHE COSA?

The phrase meaning *what?* is **che cosa?**, literally *what thing?*. Informally, Italians often use just **che?** or **cosa?**:

Che fanno?	What are they doing?
Cosa mangi?	What are you eating?

GRAMMAR GURU

A polite way to open a question is **senta scusi** (literally meaning *listen, excuse me*):

Senta scusi, dov'è il mercato per favore?	Excuse me, where is the market, please?

EXCLAMATIONS

Many of the words commonly used for forming questions can also express strong feelings as part of an exclamation.

Che bella casa!	What a beautiful house!
Che bravo ragazzo!	What a clever boy!
Quanti libri!	What a lot of books!
Quanto vino!	What a lot of wine!
Come sono cresciuti i vostri bambini!	How your children have grown!
Che vergogna!	How embarassing!
Che brutto!	How ugly!
Com'è buona questa carne!	What delicious meat!
Quante storie!	What a fuss!
Come no!	Of course!
Come mi dispiace!	I'm so sorry!

TO RECAP

- To ask a question in Italian, say the statement with a questioning tone.
- A few of the question words change endings according to gender and/or number.
- Dove + è = Dov'è (where is).
- Perché means both why? and because.
- Che cosa? (what?) can be shortened to che? or cosa?.
- Many of the question words can also be used for exclamations.

NUMBERS

NUMERAL	NUMBER IN ITALIAN
1	uno
2	due
3	tre
4	quattro
5	cinque
6	sei
7	sette
8	otto
9	nove
10	dieci
11	undici
12	dodici
13	tredici
14	quattordici
15	quindici
16	sedici
17	diciassette
18	diciotto
19	diciannove
20	venti
30	trenta
40	quaranta
50	cinquanta
60	sessanta
70	settanta
80	ottanta
90	novanta
100	cento
1,000	mille
1,000,000	un milione

TENS AND UNITS

To form numbers, you generally add the units directly after the tens: **cinquantanove** (*fifty-nine*), **ventidue** (*twenty-two*).

Ci sono venticinque alunni nella classe	There are twenty-five students in the class
Mio nonno ha novantatré anni	My grandfather is 93 years old

For the units **uno** (*one*) and **otto** (*eight*), the final vowel is dropped from the ten: **ventotto** (*twenty-eight*); **trentuno** (*thirty-one*).

Ho ventuno anni	I am 21 years old
Ci sono trentotto sedie	There are 38 chairs

ORDINAL NUMBERS

Ordinal numbers are used for ranking or ordering. In Italian, the ending changes for the feminine.

	MASCULINE	FEMININE
1st	primo	prima
2nd	secondo	seconda
3rd	terzo	terza
4th	quarto	quarta
5th	quinto	quinta
6th	sesto	sesta
7th	settimo	settima
8th	ottavo	ottava
9th	nono	nona
10th	decimo	decima

Il primo treno parte alle dieci del mattino	The first train leaves at ten in the morning
Via Mazzini è la seconda a sinistra	Mazzini Street is the second on the left

DAYS OF THE WEEK

The days of the week are not written with a capital letter in Italian:

DAY OF THE WEEK	TRANSLATION
lunedì	Monday
martedì	Tuesday
mercoledì	Wednesday
giovedì	Thursday
venerdì	Friday
sabato	Saturday
domenica	Sunday

Expressions of time do not always translate exactly. For example, the phrase *on Monday* is expressed in Italian as simply **lunedì** (*Monday*); *every Monday* as **il lunedì** (*the Monday*).

Che giorno è oggi	What day is it today?
Oggi è mercoledì	Today is Wednesday
Gioco a tennis il lunedì	I play tennis on Mondays
Andate alla festa sabato prossimo?	Are you going to the party next Saturday?
Martedì scorso sono andata dai miei genitori	Last Tuesday I went to my parents' house
L'appuntamento con il dottore è giovedì prossimo alle dieci	The doctor's appointment is next Thursday at ten
Il corso di italiano è il venerdì	The Italian class is on Fridays

MONTHS OF THE YEAR

The months are not written with a capital in Italian:

MONTH OF THE YEAR	TRANSLATION
gennaio	January
febbraio	February
marzo	March
aprile	April
maggio	May
giugno	June
luglio	July
agosto	August
settembre	September
ottobre	October
novembre	November
dicembre	December

Il mio compleanno è a febbraio	My birthday is in February

DATES

Dates are expressed in regular rather than ordinal numbers (see pp.56-57): **il ventidue giugno** (*June 22nd*); **il quattordici febbraio** (*February 14th*). The exception is the first of the month which is **il primo**: **il primo aprile** (*April 1st*).

GRAMMAR GURU

To find out the date, ask the following question:

Quanti ne abbiamo oggi? What's the date today?

The answer is expressed like this:

È il ventotto dicembre It's December 28th

TIME

You tell time in Italian by counting hours, starting with **l'una** (*one o'clock*, literally *the one*), then **le due** (*two o'clock*), **le tre** (*three o'clock*), **le quattro** (*four o'clock*), etc.

Che ore sono?	What time is it?
È l'una	It's one o'clock
Sono le undici	It's eleven o'clock
A che ora siete arrivati?	(At) what time did you arrive?
Alle cinque	At five o'clock

Times past the hour are expressed by using **e** (*and*), and times to, or before, the hour by using **meno** (*less*):

EXPRESSION OF TIME	TRANSLATION
...e un quarto	a quarter past...
...e mezza	half past...
...meno un quarto	a quarter to...
la mattina	the morning
il pomeriggio	the afternoon
la sera	the evening
mezzogiorno	noon
mezzanotte	midnight

Sono le tre del pomeriggio	It's three o'clock in the afternoon
È mezzogiorno e mezzo	It's half past twelve (noon)
Arriverà alle sei meno un quarto	He will arrive at a quarter to six

MINUTES AND HOURS

In Italian, when saying more precise times (*five past*, *ten to*, etc.), you can use **e** (*and*) or **meno** (*less*) plus the number of minutes:

Sono le nove e cinque	It's 9:05
Sono le sei e venti	It's 6:20
E' l'una meno dieci	It's ten to one
Sono le sette meno venticinque	It's twenty-five to seven

24-HOUR CLOCK

The Italians use the 24-hour clock both for official timetables and also sometimes in more general conversation. The pattern for the 24-hour clock is:

hour (1-24) + **e** + minutes (1-59)

If the time is written in numerals, the hour and minutes are separated by **h**.

24-HOUR TIME	TIME IN NUMERALS
dodici e trenta	12h30
diciassette e otto	17h08
una e cinquanta	1h50
venti e quarantacinque	20h45
undici e diciotto	11h18
ventidue	22h00

Il treno parte alle quindici e trentacinque	The train leaves at 15:35 (3:35PM)
La festa comincia alle venti	The party begins at 20:00 (8PM)
L'aereo arriva alle diciotto meno un quarto	The plane leaves at 17:45 (5:45PM)

GLOSSARY

ADJECTIVE A word such as *big* or *beautiful* that is used to describe a person, thing, or an idea.

ADVERB A word such as *quickly* or *very* that is used to describe a verb, an adjective, or another adverb.

AGREEMENT The way in which word endings change according to whether the person or thing that you are talking about is masculine or feminine, singular or plural.

COMPARATIVE A word with *er* on the end of it, such as *smaller*, *bigger*, or that has *more* or *less* before it, which is used to compare things.

CONJUGATION How the ending of a verb changes according to who is carrying out the action, and depending on whether you are referring to the past, the present, or the future.

CONJUNCTION A word such as *and* or *but* that links parts of a sentence together.

CONSONANT Any letter of the alphabet, such as *b* or *c*, that is not a vowel.

DEFINITE ARTICLE A word that means *the*.

DEMONSTRATIVE A word such as *this* or *that*, which specifies a particular person or thing.

FEMININE (FEM.) A noun, pronoun, or adjective that is classified as female rather then male.

FORMAL A polite form of language used with older people or those you do not know well.

FUTURE TENSE The form of a verb that you use to talk about events or plans in the future.

GENDER Whether a noun, pronoun, or adjective is masculine or feminine.

IMPERFECT TENSE The form of a verb that is used to describe what was happening in the past, or things that used to happen regularly.

INDEFINITE ARTICLE A word that is used to mean *a* or *an*.

INFINITIVE The basic form of a verb that you will find in a dictionary, such as *to jump*.

INFORMAL The type of language used with younger people or people you know well.

INVERSION Swapping the position of two words, such as a noun (or pronoun) and verb.

IRREGULAR VERB A verb that does not follow the usual pattern of changes (conjugation).

MASCULINE (MASC.) A noun, pronoun, or adjective that is classified as male rather then female.

NEGATIVE A statement or question in which something is not happening. It usually contains words such as *not*, *never*, *nothing*, or *no one*.

NOUN A word that is used to name an object, a person, or an abstract idea.

ORDINAL NUMBER A number such as *first* or *second* that is used to arrange a sequence of things in order or rank.

PAST PARTICIPLE Form of a verb, such as *eaten* or *watched*, that is used to form the perfect tense.

PERFECT TENSE The form of a verb used to describe events that have taken place and been completed in the past.

PLURAL Referring to more than one person, thing, or idea.

POSSESSIVE ADJECTIVE A word such as *my*, *your*, *his*, or *her* that is used with a noun to show who or what it belongs to.

PREFIX A small group of letters added to the front of a word to create a new word, such as *un* in *unhappy*.

PREPOSITION A word such *at*, *from*, *in*, or *to* that describes the position of two things in relation to each other.

PRESENT TENSE The form of a verb used to talk about what is happening now or what happens regularly.

PRONOUN A word such as *he, I, you,* or *we* that is used in place of a noun.

REFLEXIVE VERB A verb that is used with a reflexive pronoun, such as *myself* or *yourself,* as in *I wash myself.*

REGULAR VERB A verb that follows the usual pattern of changes (conjugation).

SINGULAR The form of a word that refers to a single person, thing, or idea.

STEM The main part of a verb, to which you add different endings.

SUBJECT The noun or pronoun in a sentence that is described by the verb or carries out the action to which the verb refers.

SUFFIX A letter or group of letters added to the end of a word to change its meaning, such as *s* in *houses,* or *ate* in *affectionate.*

SUPERLATIVE An adjective or adverb with *est* added to the end of it, such as *quickest,* or that has *the most* or *the least* put in front of it to compare two or more things, people, or actions.

TENSE The form of a verb that shows whether something takes or took place in the present, the past, or the future.

VERB A word such as *jump, talk,* or *have* that describes an action or a condition.

VOWEL One of the following letters of the alphabet: *a, e, i, o,* or *u.*